NONE
DARE
CALL
IT
TREASON!

BOOK 6

Presidential
Words & Deeds
&
Blatant Lies!

Robert W. Pelton
$4.95

"Treason doth never prosper,

*   "What's the reason?*

*   "Why if it prosper,*

*   "None dare call it treason."*

John Harrington

Printed in America
On Recycled Paper
In
Charleston, South Carolina

Published in America
By
The Freedom & Liberty
Foundation Press
Knoxville, Tennessee

Dedicated
To
My Beloved
America

The greatest, most generous, most benevolent and most powerful nation on the face of the earth – and the only country in the history of the world to have been founded on Biblical principles.

A nation can survive its fools, and even the ambitious. But it cannot survive treason from within.

An enemy at the gates is less formidable, for he is known and he carries his banners openly.

The traitor moves among those within the gates freely, his sly whispers rustling through the galleys, heard in the very hall of government itself.

For the traitor appears not traitor. He speaks in the accent familiar to his victims, and he wears their face and their garments, and he appeals to the baseness that lies deep in the hearts of all men.

He rots the soul of a nation - he works secretly and unknown in the night to undermine the pillars of a city - he infects the body politic so that it can no longer resist.

A murderer is less to be feared.

Cicero, 42 B.C.

CONTENTS

`

Forward

Independence Hall Where the Declaration of Independence Was Signed.

Our glorious Declaration of Independence is a timeless divinely inspired masterpiece given to mankind through the anointed pen of Thomas Jefferson.

The grand and unmatched United States Constitution is indisputably the product of Providential guidance and wisdom

13

and certainly not a document which evokes whimsical interpretations with the changing political climates.

All Americans have a moral obligation to stand up and be counted in these trying times!

Abraham Lincoln boldly declared: *"To sin by silence when they should protest, makes cowards of men."*

William Lloyd Garrison capsulized it best: *"As a free man who is determined to remain free -- I do not wish to think or speak, or write with moderation. "Tell a man whose house is on fire to give a moderate alarm; tell him to moderately rescue his wife from the hands of a ravisher; tell the mother to gradually extricate her babe from the fire into which it has fallen -- but urge me not to use moderation in a course like the present."*

Senator Barry Goldwater, 1964 Presidential candidate was castigated and verbally crucified by the media.

He simply stated this simple truism: *"Extremism in the pursuit of Liberty is no vice."*

14

This good and moral man of character soundly rocked the boat of the propagandists. He was as a result soundly defeated in the election.

The alarmed media wolves panicked the voters with their jeers and sneers and insane howls about this man's lack of *"moderation!"*

It can honestly be said that through the Providential genius of our Founding Fathers, the remaining remnants of the original American Constitutional Republic still provides more freedom, opportunity and abundance for mankind than is found in any other nation in the world.

This is true despite decade after decade of unabated treason and treachery promulgated by innumerable traitorous individuals found buried in the twiddle dee – twiddle dum administrations of both the Democrats and the Republicans.

An informed and active, not a media brainwashed electorate, is the only antidote to further prostitution of, and the ultimate destruction of, what Benjamin Franklin called our Republic.

Preface

"Treason against the United States shall consist only in levying war against them, or in adhering to their enemies, giving them aid and comfort."

U.S. Constitution. Article 111, Section 3

What is your treason I.Q.?

If you can answer the following questions, it's high.

If you miss one or more, you should read the *None Dare Call It Treason* series!

Who was behind allowing Red Chinese soldiers take airborne training at Fort Benning, Georgia?

Is this not treason?

Why was South Vietnam, South Africa, Rhodesia and numerous other American friends deliberately betrayed to the forces of evil?

Is this not treason?

Why was our friend Chiang Kai Shek not so gently coerced into a Communist dictatorship by highly placed subversives in the State Department?

Is this not treason?

Why was Cuba treasonously delivered into the clutches of Communist revolutionary Fidel Castro?

Is this not treason?

Why have untold millions of dollars consistently been used to prop up faltering Red dictatorships and to assist Communist terrorists in overthrowing non-Communist governments?

Is this not treason?

What American company sold nuclear reactors to Communist Occupied Romania?

Is this not treason?

Name the company that provided Communist Hungary with a factory designed to make 1.5 million light bulbs daily?

Is this not treason?

What well known oil company invested $1 billion for oil exploration in Communist Occupied Angola?

Is this not treason?

Can you name the American company who treasonously built and equipped a $10 million electronics plant near Warsaw for the Polish slave labor tyranny?

Is this not treason?

These are questions to which every American should rightfully have an honest answer.

Unfortunately most do not!

Tragedy was carefully orchestrated by traitors in our Government and the media with regard to Cuba, Vietnam, Laos, Cambodia, Rhodesia, China, El Salvador, Nicaragua and many other countries.

Anastasio Somoza was the former President of free Nicaragua.

He offered this startling insight in his 1980 book, Nicaragua Betrayed: *"I have factual evidence that the betrayal of Nicaragua was not perpetrated out of ignorance, but rather by design."*

Somoza was soon after assassinated!

Is this not treason?

John Lehman, Secretary of the Navy, made this shocking statement on May 25 to the 1983 Annapolis graduating class: *"Within weeks many of you will be looking across just hundreds of feet of water at some of the most modern technology ever invented in America.*

"Unfortunately, it is on Soviet ships."

Is this not treason?

Earl E.T. Smith was the American Ambassador to Cuba when it was similarly delivered to the Communists.

He makes this concise comment on July 14, 1986: *"Nicaragua is Cuba all over again."*

Can you name the company that paid the Communist dictatorship in Angola over $600 million annually in taxes and oil royalties.

This money bought new Soviet jets, tanks and helicopter gunships.

And it paid Castro for supplying 35,000 imported Cuban mercenaries who keep the Angolan people enslaved.

Is this not treason?

Stressed retired Brigadier General Andrew J. Gatsis on August 11, 1986: *"Though aware of the Communist goal of world domination, the average U.S. Citizen refuses to believe that the real threat comes from governmental officials and their non-governmental confederates who secretly espouse the same objectives as the openly avowed Communists."*

 Anthony Sutton stated in his 1986 book *The Best Enemy Money Can Buy: "We now have the formidable task of bringing these gentlemen to the bar of justice to publicly answer for their private and concealed actions."*

The *None Dare Call It Treason* series certainly won't win accolades from the United Nations or the State Department!

Nor will Harvard feel compelled to bestow an honorary degree upon the author!

Harvard Law School was the spawning ground for an incredible number of Red agents. Included were members of the first Soviet spy ring ever to be exposed in our government.

Reed Irvine aptly commented in July of 1986: *"Indeed, it has long been a joke among refugees from Eastern Europe that there are more Marxists at Harvard than there are in the Soviet Union, or Poland, or whatever Communist country the refugee called home."*

The Honorable Ezra Taft Benson said: *"The truth must be told even at the risk of destroying, in large measure, the influence of men who are widely respected and loved by the American people.*

"The stakes are high. Freedom and survival is the issue."

Treason is still a most serious federal offense.

The *None Dare Call It Treason* series examines the reasons for and the Americans behind the fall of freedom and the rise of tyranny throughout the world!

Has anything really changed?
You Decide!

Treason

Whoever, owing allegiance to the United States, levies war against them or adheres to their enemies, giving them aid and comfort within the United States or elsewhere, is guilty of treason and shall suffer death, or be imprisoned not less than five years and fined not less than $10,000; and shall be incapable of holding any office under the United states.

U.S. Code, Title 18, Section 2381

Whoever, owing allegiance to the United States and having knowledge of the commission of any treason against them, conceals and does not, as soon as may be, disclose and make known the same to the President or to some judge of the United States, or to the Governor or to some judge or justice of a particular state, is guilty of misprision of treason, and shall be fined not more than $1000 or imprisoned not more than 7 years or both.

U.S. Code, Title 18, Section 2382

Presidential

Words

&

Deeds

&

Blatant Lies!

Treason: *". . . consciously and purposely acting to aid its [one's country] enemies."*

American Heritage Dictionary

What's going on here?

One President wining and dining with the greatest mass-murdering Communist in history!

Another President authorized a national holiday to honor a black demagogue who proclaimed himself a Marxist!

One President presented a notorious security risk with a $50,000 tax-free award!

Another President delivered more than 2,000,000 people to Communist Occupied Russia for execution or for incarceration in slave labor camps!

One President protected a Communist slave labor dictatorship from invasion!

Yes, what exactly is going on here? Thomas J. Anderson aptly concluded: *"Ours is the only nation whose leaders could have done what they've done without being tried for treason."*

The Age of Treason began in the 1930s with the advent of the Roosevelt Administration!

Russian sympathizers and outright Soviet espionage agents were never in short supply during FDR's Presidential terms.

Franklin Delano Roosevelt knowingly allowed Red spies to freely infiltrate various agencies of the government! Many of them were close personal friends of his and Eleanor's!

Former Congressman Martin Dies charged: *"The Roosevelt Administration had been compromised by their collaboration with Communists and the employment of Communists in the government.*

"The Administration felt that a fearless exposure of this sordid alliance would damage the Democratic Party."

"... several of the best friends I have got are communists" said Roosevelt while accompanied by Harry

Truman when he spoke to Congressman Dies.

Roosevelt holds the unholy distinction of giving Diplomatic Recognition to Stalin's barbaric dictatorship in 1933!

This single act gave legitimacy to a small gang of thugs in Communist Occupied Russia.

He was well aware that Stalin's outlaw regime was personally responsible for murdering nearly 17 million of his own people!

 As pointed out by Representative Philip M. Crane: *"During the height of Joseph Stalin's reign of terror, more than 40,000 persons were being executed each month."*

Stalin bragged to President Truman, Winston Churchill and others as to how he had dealt with 10 million kulaks.

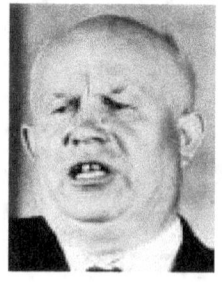 Most of these unfortunates died of forced starvation under the iron fist of Stalin's animalistic sadistic henchman Nikita Khruschev!

Such wholesale murder of Russia's most prosperous farmers didn't disturb Roosevelt in the least.

Nazi Germany and Communist Occupied Russia jointly invaded Poland in 1939.

The Red Army rounded up and methodically butchered up to 15,000 unarmed Polish military officers!

A huge pit was later discovered in the Katyn Forest near Smolensk. Here were found 12 layers of corpses in Polish military uniforms. Each man had a bullet hole in the back of his head.

Roosevelt was aware of these deliberate murders but he covered for Stalin.

George Crocker reported: *"The gruesome facts of the Katyn massacre had been laid on his desk.*

'"When documents and pictures attesting Russian guilt in the cold-blooded atrocity were brought to Roosevelt in the White House, he reacted with anger!

"Not to the Russian murders!

"But at those who had collected the facts, and he clamped the lid down tight."

An excellent example of Roosevelt's duplicity can be found in Poland's abhorrent betrayal!

FDR assured exiled Prime Minister Mikolajczyk: *"Stalin doesn't intend to take freedom from Poland. He wouldn't dare do that because he knows that the United States government stands solidly behind you. I will see to it that Poland will not be hurt in this war and will emerge strongly independent."*

The President was at the same time telling Stalin he could steal 70 thousand square miles of Polish territory!

34

Everything Roosevelt promised Mikolajczyk was an outright lie!

In 1944, Molotov revealed: *"We agreed [at the November 28 December 1, 1943, Teheran Conference] that it would be best not to issue a public declaration about our agreement."*

Roosevelt wanted his treasonous betrayal of Poland kept under wraps until after the 1944 election.

Why?

He told Stalin *"there were in the United States from six to seven million Americans of Polish extraction, and, as a practical man, he did not wish to lose their vote."*

Crass?

Yes!

Unbelievable concessions were made to the murderous Stalin at Teheran.

These promises were finalized by Roosevelt at Yalta!

And Truman at Potsdam!

Betrayal and sellout to Communism became the accepted mode of action for FDR!

It continued with all subsequent American Presidents!

Roosevelt was sick and near death when the election was held in November 1944.

Three months later a much weakened President was cleverly manipulated by Alger Hiss and his Kremlin mole Comrades.

How?

Into traveling around six thousand miles each way to attend the February 4-11, 1945 Yalta Conference!

The meeting was held in Livadia Palace built in 1911 as a vacation retreat for Czar Nicholas II.

A dying American President was a virtual prisoner of his top advisors.

The most influential of which was Kremlin spy Alger Hiss!

Roosevelt knew that Comrade Hiss had been Stalin's man since at least 1939.

. It was at this time that he'd been informed by A.A. Berle an important member of the President's *"Brain Trust"* that Alger Hiss was passing top-secret documents to the Soviets.

Yet here it was six years later and this traitor was more powerful than ever before!

Hiss stayed firmly glued to Roosevelt's side!

He was constantly whispering advice in the incapacitated President's ear.

He took care of all details.

He handled all the paperwork!

Alger Hiss was in control of President Roosevelt at Yalta!

As the painful truth about Yalta slowly emerged the extremely important role of Soviet espionage agent Alger Hiss was deliberately overlooked. Or it was deliberately played down by the government and the media!

Hiss later commented on his part: *"It is an accurate and not immodest statement to say that I helped formulate the Yalta agreement to some extent."*

Incredibly the entire sordid Yalta sellout was agreed upon two years before Roosevelt and Stalin actually got together!

Nicholas Baciu reveals how FDR wrote *"Uncle Joe on February 20, 1943, and promised the brutal Communist dictator all of the territories eventually annexed by the USSR!"*

Communist enslavement over most of Eastern and Central Europe was guaranteed!

 John T. Flynn noted that at the end of World War II FDR *"surrendered into Stalin's hands a whole collection of peoples whose land comprised, along with Russia almost two-thirds of the land mass of Europe and Asia."*

Roosevelt made a multitude of secret concessions to Stalin at Yalta.

They agreed to divide Germany!

The Russian mass-murdering psychopath was allowed the wholesale thievery of German industrial plants, factories and other property!

Millions of conquered Germans men, women, and children were to be shipped to Communist Occupied Russia!

There they were doomed to finish out their lives in barbaric slave labor concentration camps!

Stalin demanded the return of millions of Hungarians, Poles and others in Central Europe.

These were the people who'd fled since 1939!

Their only crime was having escaped from Russian controlled areas.

Westbrook Pegler revealed how Roosevelt *"made a contract with Stalin to deliver millions of European people into Russian custody as slaves.*

"It was a foregone conclusion that many of them would be killed by firing squads.

"They were Soviet subjects who had surrendered to the Nazis.

"They knew Bolshevism. They thought nothing could be worse."

The diabolical plan was officially known as *Operation Keelhaul.*

General Dwight D. Eisenhower was a Roosevelt protégé.

He willingly *"repatriated"* these helpless men, women and children against their will!

Some of the men had actually served and fought with the U.S. Army!

They too were rounded up at gun-point!

More than 2,000,000 people were herded into boxcars and shipped prepaid into the clutches of the monstrous Russian dictator!

Many committed suicide rather than return to be shot!

Or tortured!

Or to die a slower death in one of Stalin's slave-labor concentration camps.

"This surrender to their enemy of millions of prisoners of war was a crime by established law," charged Pegler. *"It was not a violation of one of the ex-post facto laws which monstrous Russians and monstrous Americans improvised against German generals and politicians for the gala hanging at Nuremberg.*

"If any of those Germans deserved hanging how about Truman, Stalin, and Ike? That ought to be the penalty for dealing in slave trade!"

Col. Ernest F. Fisher, Senior Historian, United States Army described things thusly: *"Starting in April 1945, the United States Army and the French Army casually annihilated one million [German] men, most of them in American camps.*

"Eisenhower's hatred passed through the lens of a compliant military bureaucracy produced the horror of death camps unequalled by anything in American history."

Stalin had declared that he didn't want one additional inch of real estate *"added to his empire"* as a result of the war.

U.S. guard looking over fenced off areas holding thousands of German prisoners exposed to elements.

Yet John T. Flynn charged that the diabolical monster ended up grabbing *"some 725 million people, which with the 193 million in Russia gave him dominion over 918 million human beings in Russia and 16 other European and Asiatic countries."*

Truman inherited a thoroughly Communist infiltrated executive branch.

He made no effort to change this upon becoming President!

It certainly wasn't that Truman was stupid!

He'd long been aware of the powerful Communist presence under Roosevelt.

And he knew about the multitude of subversives in his own Administration!

Prisoners of War Taken by the Russians April 1945

Not only did this man inherit all of Roosevelt's Reds.

He deliberately added a number of his own!

Truman had an ongoing romance with the Communists over a period of many years!

They even openly endorsed him for the Vice Presidency!

In return Truman the President showed complete indifference to Communist penetration at home.

President Truman went to Germany from July 17 to July 25, 1945.

This trip was made to attend the Potsdam Conference.

Here he would wheel and deal with hard-nosed Joe Stalin in implementing Roosevelt's treasonous Yalta giveaways!

Before leaving for Potsdam Truman read a report prepared by 50 top Army intelligence specialists.

They warned: *"The entry of Soviet Russia into the Asiatic War would destroy America's position in Asia.*

"China will certainly lose her independence, to become the Poland of Asia.

"Chiang may have to depart and a Chinese Soviet government may be installed."

He was then briefed by Owen Lattimore.

Lattimore had been had identified long before as a Communist spy by former *Daily Worker* editor Louis Budenz and others.

Truman totally ignored the Army intelligence report!

Prime Minister Winston Churchill, President Harry S. Truman and Communist Party General Secretary Josef Stalin shaking hands at the Potsdam Conference.

He instead followed Kremlin lackey Lattimore's Communist benefitting proposals. The Reds as could be expected accomplished *exactly* what military intelligence said they would!

Alger Hiss was able to stay close to Roosevelt and Truman!

This was even after both Presidents had been repeatedly warned by Congressman Martin Dies and J. Edgar Hoover that Alger Hiss was a Soviet spy!

When Hiss was finally *publicly* exposed as a traitor Truman, Eleanor Roosevelt, Felix Frankfurter and other powerful leftists did their best to get him off the hook!

During the 1948 election campaign, Truman charged the Hiss case was nothing more than a *"red herring."*

He was lying as could be expected!

"Red herrings" was also the phrase used by Truman to characterize the hearings of the House Committee on Un-American Activities.

This was where former Reds Whittaker Chambers and Elizabeth Bentley were testifying!

Truman knew he couldn't possibly be re-elected in 1952!

Why?

Because of his consistent *Made-In-Moscow-Policies.*

He'd been caught red-handed shielding Kremlin espionage agents!

Known Communist spies had been consistently promoted!

All congressional investigations of Reds had deliberately been blocked!

Truman completed the delivery of Eastern Europe into Stalin's bloody grip!

Chiang Kai-shek was driven out of China!

China was then delivered to Mao's Red terrorists!

Truman deliberately brought America into the Korean War with no intention of winning!

MacArthur was sacked for demanding victory!

Sanctuaries were provided for the Communist enemy!

There is much, much more.

But suffice to say Truman's sordid record spoke for itself.

In 1953 Eisenhower made his infamous *"Atoms for Peace"* speech.

This marked the beginning of the treasonous giveaway of America's nuclear research data and materials to enemy Communist regimes!

Eisenhower did more to give Communist Occupied Russia and other Red slave labor states nuclear capability than did the Rosenbergs and all other Soviet spies combined!

The Rosenberg's were sentenced to death for their traitorous deed.

Eisenhower was re-elected to another term!

On June 30, 1954, Eisenhower ignored his infamous role in the post World War 11 Operation Keelhaul.

He hypocritically proclaimed: *"I will not be a party to any agreement that makes anyone a slave."*

Was he kidding?

No!

Three weeks later, Ho Chi Minh was handed control of North Vietnam.

47

North Korean troops massacred American prisoners by making them kneel, tying their hands behind their back with barbed wire and then methodically shooting each soldier behind the head with one bullet.

Thirteen million Vietnamese people became slaves with the stroke of a pen!

Time noted: *"At Geneva the Communists got precisely what they sought; a vast slice of Indochina, and a stance from which to take the rest."*

Thanks to Eisenhower's treason America was fighting its second no-win war less than a decade later, this time in South Vietnam. Ho Chi Minh with the assistance of innumerable American traitors did *"take the rest!"*

The astounding fall of Cuba to Castro's tiny band of Communist gangsters was carefully orchestrated by Eisenhower.

The choreographed leftist scenario went like this:

Ike's subversive brother Milton met with the Red terrorist leader in his Oriente hills guerrilla hideout in November of 1958!

Castro's thugs captured Havana only six weeks later on January 1, 1959!

Diplomatic recognition was hurriedly granted to the bandit gang a week later.

Eisenhower deliberately gave Communist Occupied Russia a foothold in the Western Hemisphere!

Thanks to this President the Soviets were handed a base from which to expand their corrupt slave labor empire!

Khrushchev was invited by the President in July 1959 to visit the United States!

Yes!

Even though Ike was aware of the Butcher of Budapest's ungodly and bloody past?

Yes!

And Ike was aware of the beast's closeness to Fidel Castro?

Yes!

` Congressional hearings revealed this: *"Khrushchev personally conceived and executed*

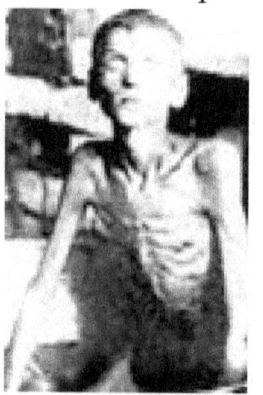

the mass starvation and liquidation of six to eight million Ukrainians in the early 1930's.

"Khrushchev was the chief executioner for the bloody Moscow purge trials in 1936.

"Khrushchev, during a second two year reign of terror in the Ukraine in 1937-38,

slaughtered another 400,000 people [including children]."

Evidently, none of this mattered to Eisenhower!

The Red carpet was dutifully rolled out at the White House for a monster who had been Stalin's most trusted henchman!

America's arch-enemy and one of the most despicable mass-murderers of all time was royally entertained at Gettysburg!

Ike's grandchildren were photographed sitting on this ghastly killer's knee!

The President called it a *"heart warming scene."*

He further declared: *"Now, I don't think that Mr. Khrushchev is himself a cruel man.*

"I'm sure he loves children.

"Oh, he's very, very much of a family man that way."

How could this American President even suggest such things?

Could he hae been that ignorant of the truth?

Not really!

Or could it have been because he was just another Comrade?

A carefully planted mole many years ago?

Is this not at least a possibility?

Will we ever really know?
Probably not!

Joseph Stalin alone was responsible for the massacre of at least 17 million persons between 1929 and 1939.

Roughly 15 million people were deliberately starved to death in the Ukraine.

By the end of 1933 nearly 25 percent of the population of the Ukraine including three million children had perished. The Kulaks as a class were destroyed and an entire nation of village farmers had been eliminated.

This equals the combined populations of over a dozen States including Idaho, Rhode Island, Delaware, and Vermont.

The ungodly deed transpired between 1932-1933 under the direction of Stalin's reprehensible Neanderthal henchman Nikita S. Khrushchev.

Khrushchev's welcome by President Eisenhower conveyed exactly what it was meant to convey.

It clearly signaled the death knell for the captive nations!

The enslaved millions behind the Iron Curtain were unmistakably being told that they could no longer hope for help from America!

Despite his acknowledged enjoyment of this Communist Neanderthal's company Ike obviously didn't feel the same way about loyal American anti-Communists.

Arthur Larson wrote: *"Toward Senator Joseph McCarthy, President Eisenhower had a sense of loathing and contempt that had to be seen to be believed."*

Eisenhower wrote that as President, I *"yearned in every fiber of my being"* to *"smash"* McCarthy.

Eisenhower would have done well to heed McCarthy's common sense warning: *"You cannot offer friendship to tyrants and murderers without advancing the cause of tyranny and murder."*

Was Eisenhower a Communist?

No one knows.

No one will probably ever know!

Historian Robert Welch drew a parallel to a politician-military man of another era – Alcibiades the Athenian traitor.

Welch offered this as food for thought: *"Alcibiades, rich, famous, honored, and powerful, was the one man most Athenians would have found it most difficult to think of as a traitor."*

The *Encyclopedia Britannica* description of Alcibiades could well fit Eisenhower: *"Superficial and opportunist to the last, he owed the successes of his meteoric career purely to personal magnetism and an almost incredible capacity for deception."*

The point isn't whether Eisenhower was or was not an agent of the Kremlin conspiracy!

Whether Ike's reasons for his actions were ideological, due to ignorance, or sheer political opportunism makes little difference!

The end result is identical.

The same is also true of every other President!

The law covering treason doesn't differentiate between ideology, ignorance and opportunism!

On January 29, 1961, President Kennedy  said: *"Let every public servant know that this Administration recognizes the value of dissent and daring, that we greet healthy controversy as the hallmark of healthy change."*

Yet forest ranger Don Caron was forced to resign in 1961 over a weekly newspaper column he was writing based on FBI reports and Congressional hearings!

The criticism given my Kennedy Administration moles?: *"The editorials reflect a zealous and almost fanatical patriotism and an active effort to awake the public to the dangers of Communism.*

"Regardless of all else, the whole subject matter is surely controversial."

Robert Strange McNamara (CFR) instituted the *Reuther Memorandum* as Kennedy's Secretary of Defense.

This radical directive was authored by the infamous leftist labor union leader Walter Reuther who once wrote from Communist Occupied Russia: *"Carry on the fight for a Soviet America."*

The incredible pro-Communist memorandum recommended the outright censorship of all military leaders!

No further criticism of Communists or Communism in speeches or writings would be tolerated!

General Edwin A. Walker had a well-deserved reputation as America's best combat officer in Europe!

He was the first major military casualty.

General Walker was relieved of his West German command in 1962.

Why?

Because he required that his men be taught patriotism!

And those soldiers are well informed about the dangers of Communism!

It was that simple!

Nothing more!

56

Security risk Adam Yarmolinsky was McNamara's hatchet-man.

He coldly axed Walker's career!

His treatment was designed to serve as a warning to other patriotic anti-Communist military officers!

It showed exactly what would happen to their careers if they spoke out against or taught anything about the Communist enemy with whom their country was at war!

Walker testified that evidently *"militant anti-Communist leadership by a division commander"* was no longer to be tolerated by Communists and other subversives in government!

At the same time the leftist *Nation* edited by Communist Carey McWilliams was allowed o be sold on American military bases for troop indoctrination!

McNamara and his *"whiz kids"* effectively enforced thought control over the opinions of military men!

Joining him in muzzling anti-Communists in the Armed Forces were such outlandish security risks as:

Secretary of State Dean Rusk.

Under Secretary of State George Ball.

and Cyrus Vance.

Advance texts of all speeches by military officers were required by a mole infested and

Communist controlled State Department censor board!

This censorship involved the deleting from speeches and writings of all unpleasant references to Communism and Communists!

Why?

Ball's illogical excuse for this traitorous activity was that *"name calling"* might be resented by the Communists!

Ball had to be joking!

But he certainly was not!

He gave specifics: the word *"slavery"* was no longer appropriate for denoting those enslaved by the Reds!

Communism was not to be referred to as *"the enemy"!*

Who then was the enemy?

Communist terrorist acts shouldn't be described as *"brutal"!*

What then were they to be called?

The Senate Armed Services Committee collected over 200 pages of anti-Communist words and remarks deleted from some of the 1500 censored speeches on hand.

In 1962, Senator Strom Thurmond gave examples of phrases blue lined from the material of Lieutenant General Arthur Trudeau.

They included:

"The steady advance of Communism".

"insidious ideology of Communism".

"The Soviets have not relented in the slightest in their determination to dominate the world and destroy our way of life."

The *Reuther Memorandum* recommended using the Internal Revenue Service.

The IRS was ordered to harass anti-Communist organizations and leaders!

 The IRS came down hard on people like widely known anti-Communist Walter Knott of Knott's Berry Farm.

Such a program was an obvious attempt to make an example out of this outspoken highly respected patriot and nationally known!

To discredit him!

To shut him up!

To drive him out of business!

To deny any and all of the legitimate tax exemptions of that had formerly been granted for his popular Southern California tourist attraction

He was wrongly assessed a fortune in back t[

Walter Knott was wrongly assessed a fortune in back taxes on technicalities and reversals of previous IRS decisions!

Whenever possible all legitimate tax exemptions were to be taken away from other anti-Communist organizations!

The IRS did this for example to anti-Communist leader Billy James Hargis and his Christian Crusade!

Why Hargis?

To stop the popular evangelist from expounding his anti-Communist rhetoric on his radio show.

It was also recommended that the Federal Communications Commission be used to eliminate anti-Communist programs from the air waves!

They succeeded!

All anti-Communist organizations were to be classed as subversive.

They to be placed on the Attorney General's list!

The Attorney General just happened to be Robert Kennedy.

Who handily enough was the brother of the President!

This recommendation was so outlandish that it was never implemented!

J. Edgar Hoover's anti-Communist activities were to be sharply reined in because he was said to *"exaggerate the domestic Communist menace"*.

He was accused of stirring up the public with regard to an internal Communist threat!

Hoover was too widely respected and admired for the Communists to curb so easily!

Never forget that all these things were initiated during the Administration of President John F. Kennedy!

Hoover spoke on dealing with the Communist threat: *"The best yardstick of the effectiveness of the fight against Communism is the fury of the smear attacks against the fighter launched and conducted by the Reds!"*

Russian missiles and long range bombers were suddenly discovered to be in Cuba!

Kennedy forced a much heralded *"eyeball to eyeball"* confrontation with Khrushchev over this..

Or so we were told by the media!

The Soviets were said to have backed down and meekly removed their missiles and planes.

But this is highly improbable.

Why?

Because the Butcher of Budapest had previously met with JFK in Vienna and boasted: *"I think that I have taught that young man what fear is!"*

No one actually saw any missiles or bombers leave Castro's concentration camp island!

Nevertheless, America-hating Marxist U Thant of the UN went to Havana during the crisis to look around.

Conveniently the man who idolized Lenin could find no missiles or big bombers!

Taking Thant's word JFK let Castro and Communist Occupied Russia conveniently slip off the hook!

No one knew it at the time but Kennedy made a secret deal with the Russian tyrant

Khrushchev in return for the purported missile removal!

On October 27, 1962, President Kennedy guaranteed the dictator of the Soviet Union that neither the U.S. nor any other nation in the Western Hemisphere would *ever* invade Communist Occupied Cuba!

The President of the United States officially made Castro's Cuba a protected Communist sanctuary!

Unbelievable as it may sound, U.S. warships were sent to patrol the Caribbean!

This was to protect the island from attack by anti-Communist Cuban exiles and refugees in the United States!

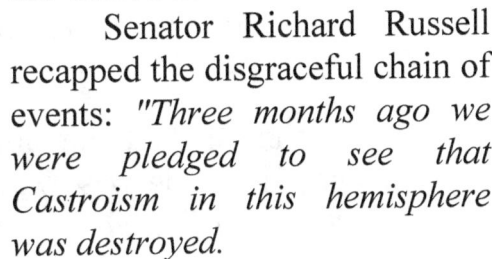

Senator Richard Russell recapped the disgraceful chain of events: *"Three months ago we were pledged to see that Castroism in this hemisphere was destroyed.*

"We have now been euchred into the position of baby-sitting for Castro and guaranteed the integrity of the Communist regime in Cuba.

"We don't know for a fact that the missiles and bombers have been removed.

"All we have seen is a box they said contained a bomber and a long metal container that they said contained a missile.

"We have not had on-the-spot inspection. "

Lyndon Baines Johnson was an ambitious, dishonest and corrupt politician.

This pseudo-conservative sounded like an English speaking Karl Marx in 1964.

He bluntly declared his intent as President: *"We are going to take all the money that we think is unnecessarily being spent and take it from the 'haves' and give it to the 'have nots' who need it so much. "*

Johnson had previously announced that he was *"further to the left than Eleanor Roosevelt. "*

The much heralded *"War on Poverty"* was launched under LBJ's Presidency.

Harvard clone former Young Communist League member Adam Yarmolinsky (CFR) of Harvard teamed up with Daniel P. Moynihan to write the *Act* that created the Office of Economic Opportunity!

The agency immediately as was intended became a watering hole for Communist agitators, known moles and far-left radicals!

The Soviet ship Anosov leaving Cuba, November 6, 1962. It was *said* but never proven to be carrying a cargo of 8 missiles to be returned to the Soviet Union!

Revolutionaries employed in the OEO distributed money to their revolutionary counterparts in the streets!

Innumerable *War on Poverty* grants were used to finance their Communist directed activities!

For example, Leroi Jones Black Arts Repertory Theater in New York City received a great deal of cash from the OEO.

Run by this black revolutionary, the basement was headquarters for black terrorists who specialized in murdering other blacks!

Pure and simple, Lyndon Johnson was guilty of treasonously financing Communist revolutionary activity in the streets of America!

In 1954, the Atomic Energy Commission pulled Dr. J. Robert Oppenheimer's security clearance.

He was denied access to classified government data.

The AEC found that Oppenheimer, director of the A-bomb project during WW II *"was not a mere 'parlor pink' but was deeply and consciously involved with hardened and militant Communists at a time when he was a man of mature judgment.*

"His relations with these hardened Communists were such that they considered him to be one of their number."

Oppenheimer had been on the Communist-founded ACLU's National Committee since 1948!

His wife, mistress and brother were all Communists.

He regularly gave money to the Party and attended meetings!

William L. Borden who was the former Executive Director of the Joint Committee on Atomic Energy concluded: *"More probably than not, J. Robert Oppenheimer is an agent of the Soviet Union."*

In December 1963, Lyndon Johnson presented this subversive with the AEC's prestigious Enrico Fermi award.

Oppenheimer walked away with a tax-free $50,000 check!

A month later, Johnson shamelessly honored the notorious Marxist Roger Baldwin on his 80th birthday.

This subversive was a long-time Communist Fronter and a founder of the infamous ACLU!

His wife Madeline Doty was a courier for the Bolshevists!

Baldwin boldly testified before Congress that he upheld an alien's right to *"advocate the overthrow of the government by force and violence"* and to *"advocate murder and assassination."*

Writing in a Harvard class reunion book: *"I am for Socialism, disarmament, and ultimately for abolishing the State itself. Communism is the goal."*

The President hypocritically told this anti-American leftist: *"Your unremitting fight against injustice and intolerance in this country has earned you the warm gratitude of countless individuals.*

"You have shown a devotion to principle which will long be remembered by your countrymen."

Johnson never deviated from the Kennedy policy of banning the sale of arms and military hardware to South Africa -- a free anti-Communist country!

And a reliable American ally!

South Africa was treated as if it were a despicable slave state!

And a threat to U.S. security!

This same hypocrite traitorously opened the floodgates to supply Communist slave labor dictatorships throughout the world with food and arms.

"The Chinese Communists are international criminals!" said Richard M. Nixon a Presidential candidate in 1968.

He wouldn't agree to let Red China join the UN!

Nor would he allow trade with them!

Nevertheless by 1971 Nixon the President had done away with all trade restrictions regarding those *"international criminals."*

He enthusiastically endorsed Red China's admission to the UN.

Nixon the President then engineered a stunning reversal of long standing U.S. policy.

He and his subversive shadow the sinister Kremlin agent Henry *"Bor"* Kissinger made a traitorous pilgrimage to Communist Occupied China in 1972.

This visit will forever stand as one of the most monstrous sellouts in all history.

Here a leader of the greatest nation the world has ever known was toasting one of the worst atheistic mass-murderers of the era!

Nixon obsessively sought a new relationship with Communist Occupied China's maniacal despots!

The President cold-bloodedly served up South Vietnam for sacrifice in a graceless show of treachery!

He ruthlessly plunged a knife in the back of America's old friend and long-term ally the Nationalist Chinese Government on Taiwan.

Chou En-lai required these things as tribute before he would allow Nixon to visit his Red slave dictatorship.

All of this and more was part of the sordid package deal identified Soviet spy Henry *"Bor"* Kissinger had previously arranged with Chou.

Uncomplimentary terms were to be avoided!

Included were:

"planned famines"
"forced abortions"
"slave labor"
"genocide"
"terrorist acts"
"mass murderers" etc.

Upwards of 50 million people had been killed in Red China since 1957.

They were no longer referred to in Washington circles as *"murderous atrocities"*.

Such mass murder was now to be politely referred to as no more than a *"population setback!"*

Nixon's Secretary of the Army Stanley R. Resor authorized a controversial directive on dissent.

This order was sent to all military commanders throughout the world.

The directive was blatantly pro-Communist.

It could easily have been written by some wild-eyed Communist propagandist working for Russia's *Izvestia* and *Pravda*.

Yet its authors worked in the Pentagon!

Included were these incredible guidelines:

73

Commanding officers can't punish military personnel who work on Communist projects off post!

Why?

Communist indoctrination centers usually called coffee houses can't be placed off limits to servicemen!

Why?

Servicemen can't be banned from distributing Communist literature on base or off!

Why?

The purchase or possession of Red literature on the base can't be prohibited!

Why?

The United States issued the *Monroe Doctrine* in 1823.

This stated that any attempt by a European power to reassert control over a rebellious colony in South America would be viewed as a threat to the United States.

Nixon deliberately ignored the *Monroe Doctrine*!

When?

This took place when Chile became another Communist dictatorship in this hemisphere!

The leftist media offered no protest!

Nixon deliberately ignored Peru when U.S. property was seized and the little country became a Marxist tyranny!

The leftist media said nothing!

Nixon deliberately ignored the Communist coup in Ecuador!

The leftist media said little!

Nixon made it *"perfectly clear"* that he had no intention of defending Panama even in the event of a Soviet backed invasion!

This despite the fact that the Panama Canal was by treaty made U.S. property *"in perpetuity"*.

This was required as a condition for Congressional approval to finance the canal's construction.

Nixon met with Soviet Leonid Brezhnev and then traitorously wrote off the Captive Nations in Europe and Asia!

The treasonous Nixon Doctrine supported *"the legalization of Communist control over all people and nations seized during and since World War II."*

Nixon officially accepted the legitimacy of the Red slave states!

He thereby abandoned millions of Europeans to a hopeless life of hardship and misery!

Ford was the President who guaranteed Communist Occupied Russia's permanent enslavement of the Captive Nations in Eastern Europe!

How?

This was accomplished in 1975 when he signed the European Security Agreement in Helsinki.

By partaking of this treachery Ford ratified the Roosevelt-Hiss treacherous sellout of Poland, Romania, Yugoslavia and other Soviet satellite countries!

Ford also agreed that Russia would permanently occupy East Germany!

 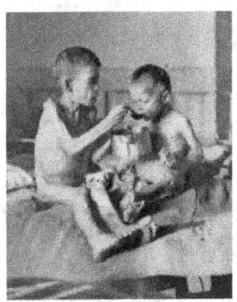

This is all quite interesting especially since each of our Presidents had to be aware of how the Soviet Union had deliberately planned a famine in the Ukraine.

This was no secret!

Or how when resistance developed the Soviets deliberately infected the women of entire villages with venereal diseases!

Medical treatment was denied unless these women informed on everyone who was involved in the anti-Russian movement.

President Ford continued *all* of Nixon's leftist programs.

He also retained most of the Nixon's radical leftist appointees.

Ford made it clear immediately after being sworn in that there'd be *no* changes in foreign policy.

This of course simply meant a continuation of Kissinger's program of retreat, humiliation, disarmament, surrender and betrayal!

And Kissinger was a man who'd long ago been exposed as a Communist spy in the employ of the Soviet Union.

One of Ford's betrayals was the dismantling America's $6 billion Anti-Ballistic Missile system *one month* after it became operational!

Meanwhile, the Soviet Union installed their American-designed ABM system.

It was run by computers supplied by Control Data Corporation and IBM.

Foreign Affairs was the house organ of the Council on Foreign Relations.

This radical publication sounded as it were an official Communist propaganda journal when it called for the *liberation* of Mozambique and Angola!

Also demanded was a *"swamp of blood"* in South Africa!

Gerald Ford tried his best to accomplish all three of these demands!

This President wouldn't consider liberating Communist slave labor dictatorships

Yet he avidly sought to destroy free anti-Communist nations!

Was he simply ignorant?

Or was it all by design?

Soviet moles throughout the Ford Administration completed the betrayal of Mozambique to Communist terrorists in late 1974!

They delivered Angola to the Reds in 1975!

And they allowed the Communist controlled Organization of African Unity to funnel American tax dollars to Red terrorist groups!

One of which who happened to be waging a brutal war against the free people of a reliable American friend anti-Communist South Africa!

Ford did his dead level best to destroy Ian Smith's anti-Communist Rhodesia!

And to turn it over to Red revolutionaries!

He declared: *"The United States is totally dedicated to seeing to it that the majority [black] becomes the ruling power in Rhodesia."*

Ford was no more than a hypocritical meddler.

He wasn't at all dedicated to forcing a similar majority rule on such Communist slave labor dictatorships as:

Russia.
China.
Cuba.
Vietnam.
Poland.
Hungary, etc.

Why?

elections in 1976.

Gerald Ford wanted as did Richard Nixon before him to treasonously give away the Panama Canal.

The American-owned canal was to be turned over to the tinhorn Communist dictator in Panama.

The treachery was to be culminated right after the

It was President Jimmy Carter rather than President Gerald Ford who ended up committing the treason!

Carter was the *only* American President to be photographed giving the Communist clenched-fist salute!

His radical leftist behavior was noted at an Atlanta victory celebration: *"Carter symbolically clenched his fist and held it high."*

Every newspaper in the U.S. carried a photograph of KGB trained Kremlin Assassin Lee Harvey Oswald giving an identical salute after he'd been captured!

Such a gesture is universally recognized as the Communist sign denoting violent aggression.

Immediately after taking office in January, 1977, Carter halted all SR-71 reconnaissance flights over Communist Occupied Cuba!

Castro's island fortress was somehow determined to be a *"low priority"* area!

This conclusion was reached by the Carter Administration despite the fact that the Soviet Union was shipping their Cuban clone every imaginable kind of military hardware including missiles!

Carter withdrew *all* U.S. agents operating covertly inside Communist Occupied Russia!

Carter treasonously suppressed the 1979 discovery of a Russian combat brigade stationed in Cuba!

He even accepted Castro's Communist dictatorship as no more than the *"toleration of ideological diversity."*

Carter shockingly announced that there'd be no proclamation honoring Captive Nation's Week in 1977!

The gutless wonder didn't wish to offend Communist Occupied Russia!

How?

By drawing attention to their string of slave labor tyrannies!

Carter further betrayed America's dependable Free Chinese allies by canceling the *Mutual Defense Treaty*!

 Taiwan was denied the purchase of jet fighter planes and other military goods essential to their survival.

One of Carter's most despicable acts was to more closely ally the United States with Peking's mass-murderers.

He granted Diplomatic Recognition to Red China's horrid dictatorship in 1979.

This to a regime known to have methodically eliminated as many as 64 million of its own people.

It happened in the three short decades after the Communist enslavement of this hapless nation.

Most Favored Nation trade status was also given to Communist Occupied China.

This dictatorship maintains more than 7,500 concentration camps filled with 23 million or more slave laborers!

Carter developed and utilized a pretentious *"human rights"* scheme throughout his term of office.

It was an efficient means of undermining and destabilizing the governments of long-term anti-Communist allies!

All of these pro-American nations were under siege by Soviet-and Cuban-supported Red terrorists!

Nicaragua.

Argentina.

Brazil.

Guatemala.

Paraguay.

Uruguay.

Chile.

Any reasonable and necessary military response to terrorist violence was hypocritically called by Carter a *"violation of human rights"*.

The same is true when Communist revolutionaries were jailed for kidnapping, bombings and murder!

The horrendous terrorist acts themselves were completely and deliberately overlooked!

On April 1, 1977, as if participating in a monstrous April fool joke Communist Occupied Russia demanded a stop to all criticism of them regarding human rights!

They audaciously charged it was *"interference in Soviet internal affairs."*

Carter meekly obeyed!

On the other hand an arms embargo was ordered against America's ally South Africa on October 27, 1977!

Carter the consummate hypocrite claimed there was a *"blatant deprivation of basic human rights"* in South Africa!

Shandong No. 2 Labor Re-education Camp in Zibo is also a carbonized thermal parts factory. All inmates are expected to do factory work or manual labor. The camp is one of more than 300 special prisons in China.

Warranted censure of the slave labor concentration camp filled Russian dictatorship ceased!

Unwarranted criticism intensified of South Africa and Rhodesia.

Both countries were free non-slave labor republics without concentration camps.

Major General John K Singlaub reminded the President: *"We in the Free World must recognize that the subjugated peoples of the*

enslaved and captive nations of the world-wide Communist Empire are one of the potentially most powerful forces in the world.
"They are, in fact, our strongest ally and constitute our greatest opportunity to bring the dismemberment of the Communist Empire without the risks of nuclear holocaust."

Carter induced Somalia to break relations with Communist Occupied Russia and toss the Soviets out of their Berbera military base.

Somalia knowing no better became an eager ally of the U.S.

Prodded by Carter, they invaded Ethiopia in an attempt to overthrow the weak Communist tyranny.

Carter then proceeded to betray the heroic little anticommunist country!

He refused to supply it with fuel, weapons, and military hardware as promised!

The Somalian Army was soundly defeated!

Carter's National Security Council under Marxist Brzezinski adopted *Presidential Review Memorandum No. 10.*

This memo advocated giving one-third of West Germany to Communist Occupied Russia should they invade Western Europe.

Carter deliberately betrayed this long-time  friend and ally Iran although it was of great geopolitical importance to the United States.

Political analyst Hilaire duBerrier declared: *"Anyone who wishes to believe that Jimmy Carter destroyed the Shah of Iran out of naiveté is of course free to do so."*

Guerrillas from Communist Occupied Nicaragua and Red Cuba ferociously attacked Guatemala.

Carter cut off military assistance to the Guatemalan anti-Communists!

Why?

 The Georgia peanut farmer said the the Sandinistas were nothing more than idealistic and harmless *"agrarian reformers."*

Could President Carter have been this uninformed?

He had to know better!

After all these were the exact words used by Kremlin moles in our government to so wrongly describe the Red terrorists who captured free China some years ago.

Was this simply a coincidence?

Of course not!

$75 million was given to the gangster leaders of the Nicaraguan police state in mid-September 1980!

According to Carter, no intelligence data indicated that the Reds were exporting their violent revolution to other parts of Latin America.

The President lied!

Representative William Young was a member of the House Intelligence Committee.

He said: *"Intelligence reports confirm in overwhelming detail that the Sandinista clique is engaged in the export of violence and revolution.*

"There is no disagreement within the Intelligence Community on the evidence."

Daniel Ortega was

no more than another Kremlin stooge.

This Red gangster ordered the execution of hundreds of thousands of his countrymen following the July 1979 occupation of Nicaragua by his fellow Communist terrorists!

His brother Humberto warned that enemies of the Red regime *"will be hanging along the roads and highways of the country."*

Despite this the Georgia peanut farmer enthusiastically welcomed this corrupt little thug to the White House!

Madison Avenue Danny came on September 24, 1979.

He must have chuckled to himself upon finding such an abundance of groveling Carter people.

They were stumbling all over themselves to shake his bloody hand!

The whole event was an embarrassment to the American people!

Carter absurdly made Ortega an offer to train his Communist soldiers on U.S. military bases in Panama!

The designer sunglass-clad little dictator turned down this asinine proposal!

He was no doubt in shock!

Why should he bother sending his troops to train in Panama?

Soviet, Cuban and East German *"advisors"* were already training them in Nicaragua?

The unilateral disarming of the U.S. was continued by Carter!

For example, hundreds of millions of dollars were wasted when Minuteman missile production was canceled!

Incredibly the facilities as well as the tooling were destroyed so the program couldn't be reinstituted!

So rabidly was the Carter disarmament clique performing its task that retired Air Force General Ira Eaker couldn't recall the approval of any weapons recommended by the Joint Chiefs of Staff!

Recommendations on the other hand coming from Russia's Howdy Doody look alike Party boss Leonid Brezhnev fared much better.

According to Eaker, Brezhnev wanted Carter to cancel the B-1 Bomber program.

Carter canceled!

The Russians meanwhile were aggressively pursuing their own bomber building program!

He wanted the U.S. to stop building a nuclear aircraft carrier.

Carter stopped!

Brezhnev expressed dissatisfaction with the MX missile, the neutron bomb and the cruise missile.

Carter delayed them all!

The Carter betrayal list is incredible!

He praised Julius Nyerere the barbaric dictator of Communist Occupied Tanzania.

Carter fondly called this ghastly Red terrorist a *"superb politician"* who *"recognizes that the structure of government can be used for beneficial purposes."*

Was the President referring to Nyerere's one party police state, wanton torture and murder of all political opposition?

Or the slave labor camps set up to hold the *"relocated"* half of Tanzania's population?

Ronald Reagan campaigned for the Presidency as a fiery anti-Communist conservative in 1980.

Yet he did absolutely nothing to correct the critical lack of internal security safeguards upon becoming President!

He befriended and assisted and fed and armed Communist tyrants from

Poland to Afghanistan.

Yugoslavia to Angola.

And Romania to Zimbabwe.

He continued to make unreasonable demands of anti-Communist South Africa.

This was a free country, a reliable ally and a long term friend to the United States.

Let's not forget that it was under Reagan's leadership when unarmed American marines were murdered by terrorists in Lebanon!

These fighting men hadn't been allowed to carry loaded guns while on sentry duty!

Reagan did an astounding about face when he treasonously abandoned another staunch American ally the anti-Communist Republic of China on Taiwan!

He instead callously recognized the Communist People's Republic of China as the sole legal government of China.

Reagan made a pilgrimage to blood-soaked Communist Occupied China as did Presidents before him.

On October 23, 1983, the US marine barracks in Beirut, Lebanon was blown up by a suicide bomber driving a truck loaded with explosives. 241 unarmed Marines died.

He proceeded to toast the greatest mass-murderers of our age!

This purported anti-Communist President greatly expanded aid to and trade with the criminal Chinese Reds.

Reagan enthusiastically began to modernize the Communist Chinese military.

He approved of financing Red Chinese trade with low interest loans from the Export-Import Bank.

The Communist Sandinista gangsters

weren't placed in office by a popular vote of the people!

Nor had their oppressive dictatorship been ratified by the people!

Yet leftists of every hue from pink to red complained that the U.S. was trying to overthrow the *duly constituted* government of Communist Occupied Nicaragua!

By whom exactly was this Red tyranny *duly constituted*?

Even Reagan refused to drive the Communists out of Nicaragua!

Although Ortega was known to be running a hostile armed camp only a two-day drive from the United States!

The President made these incredible statements: *"But let us be clear as to the American attitude toward the government of Nicaragua.*

"We do not seek its overthrow."

Why not?

"We do not seek the military overthrow of the Sandinista government."

On April 28, 1984, Deng Xiaoping Chairman of the Advisory Committee of Central Committee of the Communist Party of China met President Reagan in the Great Hall of the People in Beijing.

Why not?

That's the only reason there's conflict in Central America in the first place!

The Red dictatorship in Managua intended to eventually help overthrow the United States Government!

Robert d'Aubuisson wanted to set up a constitutional government in El Salvador.

It was to be modeled after the United States.

He wanted to govern El Salvador by implementing the 1980 Republican Platform.

Incredibly Reagan rejected him as a *"devious rightwing fanatic"*!

Crypto-Communist Napoleon Duarte was a known by the Reagan Administration to be a Marxist.

His ideology was no secret!

Nevertheless this man was falsely labeled a *"moderate"*!

He was thereby given the support of the Kremlin mole infested and controlled State Department.

This was no more than a bit of trickery designed to fool the American citizenry

Reagan authorized a CIA expenditure of $2 million to buy the election for Duarte.

This took place   despite the fact that Duarte was known an ally of the very Communist terrorists who were supposed to be his deadly foes!

Mozambique's Samora Machel was welcomed in September of 1985.

Marxist Machel was wined and dined and toasted in Washington despite the fact he was a notorious terrorist!

And a practicing cannibal as well!

This contemptible criminal set up untold numbers of slave labor concentration camps to keep his people in line!

The doors of the Reagan White House were thrown open to enemies of freedom all over the globe!

Reagan became the epitome of the crass politician.

How?

When he signed rather than vetoed legislation for a national holiday commemorating the birthday of Marxist agitator Martin Luther King!

 Congressman John Ashbrook was the ranking minority member of the House Committee On Un-American Activities.

He charged that King had *"done more for the Communist Party than any other person of this decade."*

King was trained, supported and advised by known Communists!

King's top aid was radical leftist Andrew Young.

This man may have been a Kremlin mole.

It would have surprised no one in intelligence circles!

This dangerous leftist later became President Carter's Ambassador to the United Nations.

And the Mayor of Atlanta.

He and Young were both trained at Tennessee's subversive Highlander Folk School.

It was cited as a Communist training facility and as *"a meeting place for known Communists or fellow travelers."*

Might it not be late in the game when a national holiday is named in honor of a Red-associated demagogue?

This was a man unstable enough to have at least twice attempted suicide.

He was widely known to be a notorious bedroom athlete.

The FBI had recordings covering many of his sexual escapades.

He was a leftist whose subversive record was hidden from the public by a January 31, 1977, court order!

He was a revolutionary who was an important cog in the conspiracy to replace the government of the United States with a Kremlin directed dictatorship?

He was a radical quoted by the FBI as declaring, *"I am a Marxist!"*

And he was a racist who may well have been a Communist espionage agent himself?

King's Southern Christian Leadership Conference was misnamed.

Try Southern Communist Leadership Conference!

It had been founded and run for years by Communist organizer Bayard Rustin.

Rustin had been convicted in 1953 of sex perversion in Pasadena, California.

The SCLC's Executive Director and close King advisor was Hunter Pitts *"Jack"* O'Dell.

This Red was a Party organizer in New Orleans and on the National Committee of the Communist Party USA!

O'Dell later became Jesse Jackson's foreign policy advisor in the Presidential campaigns of

1984 and 1988!

King's other trusted advisor was New York attorney Stanley David Levison.

Andrew Young said Levison was *"one of the closest friends Martin Luther King ever had."*

Levison handled the distribution of cash subsidies provided by Communist Occupied Russia for the Communist Party in the United States!

He was in frequent contact with KGB agent Viktor M. Lessiovski!

When King died Levison became an advisor to UN Ambassador Andrew Young.

And to his successor leftist Donald McHenry as well!

Reagan's reaction was shocking when a Soviet fighter plane deliberately shot down Korean 007 airliner on September 1, 1983.

Congressman Larry McDonald and 268 other civilians were allegedly killed in this calculated terrorist act!

Here's an interesting sidelight to the story!

According to Federal Aviation Administration spokesman Orville Brockman at FAA headquarters in Washington, D.C.: *"Japanese self-defense force confirms that the Hokkaido radar followed Air Korea to a landing in Soviet territory on the island of Sakhalinska."*

The above statement was heard by this author only one time on a major television news program.

Any reference to this controversial comment was never heard again.

Why?

What happened to such an important piece of news?

Who could have squelched this incredible story?

But squelch it someone in a powerful position did!

The leadership of Communist Occupied Russia insultingly referred to McDonald as *"a bush league McCarthy"*.

These infamous international criminals charged that he was *"notorious for his virulent anti-Communism and strict tab-keeping on left and progressive organizations."*

All McDonald did was regularly expose Communists and fellow travelers in his speeches, in committee testimony and in the *Congressional Record.*

Yet Ronald Reagan was evidently fearful of offending the vicious Soviet Bear!

He avoided mentioning McDonald by name in public pronouncements concerning the merciless attack!

It was simply business as usual.

Arms giveaways continued non-stop!

So did massive grain sales.

Unlimited loans. The building of factories, etc.

107

One moment Reagan blasted Communist Occupied Russia as *"an evil empire."*

The next he'd be joking with wiley dictator Mikhail Gorbachev.

The President offered new trade agreements to give the enemy more food, technology and weapons!

He rightfully accused the Soviets of sponsoring terrorists and terrorism throughout the world.

Without skipping a heartbeat Reagan offered the Reds even more dangerous disarmament concessions!

During the Presidential campaign Walter Mondale (CFR) promised to cut the defense budget by $103 billion over a three year span between 1986 and 1989.

Once in office, Reagan reversed himself and greatly outdid his opponent!

He okayed a defense cut of *$124 billion* over a two year period between 1986 and 1988!

Reagan stressed the need to rearm the United States.

Instead the dismantling of many weapons systems was accelerated!

He cut back on building the Trident submarine.

The Polaris/Poseidon nuclear submarine was delayed indefinitely even as Reagan warned

Americans of the dangerous Soviet military threat.

The humbers of MX missiles were drastically reduced!

He refused to deploy the Minuteman III missiles!

B-62 Bombers were deactivated!

Another of Reagan's reprehensible acts was his actions with regard to the *United Nations Genocide Treaty*.

So controversial is this treaty that is had consistently been rejected since first being presented to the Senate by Truman in 1949!

This dangerous treaty subjects Americans to trial and prosecution in *international courts*!

And by foreign tribunals in violation of our *Constitution*!

The treaty also places U.S. sovereignty and civil liberties at the whim of the anti-American Communist controlled UN.

To read the facts about the founding of this incredibly dangerous organization get a copy of *None Dare Call It Treason Book 15*.

It's titled *The House That Hiss Built! The Anti-American United Nations!*

The book is a mind boggling expose of that Godless Marxist organization.

Throwing the weight of the Presidency behind Senate ratification of this treaty charged Clifford Barker, was *"one of the most monumental acts of betrayal ever committed against the United States."*

President Reagan's dynamic conservative rhetoric notwithstanding, he essentially pursued the worn out socialistic New Deal policies of Roosevelt and Truman!

Traitorous collaboration with Communist Occupied Russia continued!

Eisenhower's coddling of exposed Red moles continued unabated!

Kennedy's dismantling of U.S. defenses continued!

Johnson's blatant arming of the enemy continued!

Nixon's appeasement and surrender posture continued!

Carter's unrelenting sellout of America's strategic interests continued!

The *"conservative"* President's eight year record speaks for itself!

Was Ronald Reagan a helpless captive of the establishment left?

Or was he merely a cynical actor who all along unquestionably knew exactly what he was doing?

His record speaks for itself!

Does it not?

You decide.

Epilogue

The record covering crucial episodes of the McCarthy era has been massively and deliberately distorted from the very beginning!

Conveniently forgotten or deliberately overlooked are the 78 hearings held between 1951 and 1952 by Senator William E. Jenner's (R-Indiana) Senate Internal Security Subcommittee (SISS); the House Committee On Internal Security; the House Un-American Activities Committee (HUAC) under the chairmanship of both Martin Dies (D-Texas) and Francis Walters (D-Pa); the Federal Bureau of Investigation (FBI) under the guidance of J. Edgar Hoover; and other investigating committees and individuals.

Out of all of these investigations one man was selected:

To be stopped!

To be destroyed!

To be made an example!

Why?

So that no one would ever again dare to initiate any investigations into the penetration of our government agencies by communist agents (spies) in the employ of the Soviet Union!

Yes!

An obscure Senator from Wisconsin was deliberately targeted for this purpose!

Joseph McCarthy's incredibly successful investigations panicked those on the political left.

Their reaction was shockingly quick!

Key data was been suppressed, denied and even widely falsified.

This took place in the media, all branches of government and many alleged scholars entrenched in the ivory towers of our institutions of higher learning!

Such misreporting and misrepresentation of the facts continues today.

Much of the misinformation we were (and still are today) so carefully spoon-fed about Senator Joseph McCarthy the man and his investigations was no more than an admixture of uncheckable blovations from deceased third parties and demonstratable falsehoods!

For example, how many innocent people were harmed by McCarthy's revelations?

The correct answer?

Not one!

No!

Not One!

McCarthy's most virulent critics have had more than a half century to produce the names of the hundreds of innocent people they claim were destroyed by the astounding revelations of the Senator from Wisconsin.

Yet those highly skilled propagandists in our media and government and institutions of higher learning have been unable to name even one innocent person they claim was destroyed after being falsely accused by McCarthy!

How many innocent people committed suicide as a result of McCarthy's exposure?

The correct answer?

Not one!

Not one suicide can be attributed to the investigations conducted by McCarthy!

No! Not one!

According to the obscene claims made the highly skilled propagandists in our media, government and scholars entranced in those ivory towers of our colleges and universities there were a rash of suicides with bodies falling constantly of the heads of pedestrians below on the streets of Manhattan!

Once again, McCarthy's most virulent critics have had more than 50 years to produce the names of the hundreds of innocent people they claim committed suicide because of the astounding revelations of the Senator from Wisconsin.

Yet those highly skilled propagandists in our media and government and institutions of higher learning have been unable to name even one innocent person they claim committed suicide after being falsely accused by McCarthy!

No!

Not one!

But there were two suicides on record during the McCarthy period!

Neither was the result of an innocent person who'd been ruined by McCarthy's revelations!

Both were subversives who'd been exposed by McCarthy!

Both were subversives who'd been positively indentified as Kremlin agents!

Lawrence Duggan had been operating in the State Department as a widely known Soviet spy!

He'd been called to testify before a Congressional investigating committee.

Duggan never made it!

He conveniently "fell" from a window high up in a Manhattan skyscraper!

Fell?

Probably not!

He was more than likely pushed from or tossed out of the window by an assassin in the employ of the Soviet Union!

Why?

To make certain he didn't fold under pressure and start naming other Kremlin moles.

Secondly there was the unexpected demise of Harry Dexter White.

This Soviet agent discovered that he was being investigated by J. Edgar Hoover of the FBI!

He died of a sudden heart attack!

Coincidence?

Not hardly!

Was White's death a suicide?

Yes or at least so claimed McCarthy's critics!

Again, not hardly!

Heart attacks can readily be induced with the proper use of certain medicines administered by a hired assassin in the employ of the Kremlin!

Why?

Simply to eliminate anyone who might panic and decide to turncoat and reveal the names of other spies secretly entrenched deeply in the bowels of every branch of our government.

To sum up, most fit into one of three categories:

Conscience lacking incurable liars!
Those with an axe to grind!
Individuals who simply do not know the facts!

If you liked this book in the *None Dare Call It Treason* series then you'll probably also enjoy reading the others!

Gift copies of this book can be ordered at

robertwpelton.com or Amazon.com

Available Titles

None Dare Call It Treason Book 1
The Internal Security Farce!
5.5" x 8.5" 97 pages $4.95
Order from robertwpelton.com
or Amazon.com

None Dare Call It Treason Book 2
Never Ending Subversion In Government!
5.5" x 8.5" 202 pages $4.95
Order from robertwpelton.com
or Amazon.com

None Dare Call It Treason Book 3
*America's Subversive State Department
Bloated With Security Risks*
5.5" x 8.5" 202 pages $4.95
Order from robertwpelton.com
or Amazon.com

None Dare Call It Treason Book 4
America's Illustrious State Department!
It's Machiavellian Misdeeds!
5.5" x 8.5" 202 pages $4.95
Order from robertwpelton.com
or Amazon.com

None Dare Call It Treason Book 5
Our Presidents A Major Security Threat!
5.5" x 8.5" 202 pages $4.95
Order from robertwpelton.com
or Amazon.com

None Dare Call It Treason Book 6
Presidential Words & Deeds &Blatant Lies!
5.5" x 8.5" 202 pages $4.95
Order from robertwpelton.com
or Amazon.com

None Dare Call It Treason Book 7
Subversives Close To Our Presidents
5.5" x 8.5" 89 pages $4.95
Order from robertwpelton.com
or Amazon.com

None Dare Call It Treason Book 8
Henry Kissinger
The Shadowy Untouchable Kremlin Spy!
5.5" x 8.5" 202 pages $4.95
Order from robertwpelton.com
or Amazon.com

None Dare Call It Treason Book 9
Inexcusably Arming America's Enemies!
5.5" x 8.5" 202 pages $4.95
Order from robertwpelton.com
or Amazon.com

None Dare Call It Treason Book 10
Inexcusably Financing
America's Enemies!
5.5" x 8.5" 202 pages $4.95
Order from robertwpelton.com
or Amazon.com

None Dare Call It Treason Book 11
Treasonous   Trade With & Aid To
Enemies Of Freedom!
5.5" x 8.5" 202 pages $4.95
Order from robertwpelton.com
or Amazon.com

None Dare Call It Treason Book 12
Wholesale Treason During the War
In Vietnam!
5.5" x 8.5" 202 pages $4.95
Order from robertwpelton.com
or Amazon.com

None Dare Call It Treason Book 13
Big Business & Astounding Acts Of Treason!
5.5" x 8.5" 202 pages $4.95
Order from robertwpelton.com
or Amazon.com

None Dare Call It Treason Book 14
Illegally Importing Slave Made Goodies!
5.5" x 8.5" 202 pages $4.95
Order from robertwpelton.com
or Amazon.com

None Dare Call It Treason Book 15
The House That Hiss Built
The Anti-American United Nations!
5.5" x 8.5" 202 pages $4.95
Order from robertwpelton.com
or Amazon.com

None Dare Call It Treason Book 16
Security Risks in the House and Senate!
5.5" x 8.5" 202 pages $4.95
Order from robertwpelton.com
or Amazon.com

None Dare Call It Treason Book 17
*The Supreme Court A Devastating
Threat To National Security!*
5.5" x 8.5" 202 pages $4.95
Order from robertwpelton.com
or Amazon.com

Orders for Resale
40% Off Retail Price

Send Purchase Order to

christianamerica2@yahoo.com

MEET THE AUTHOR

Robert W. Pelton has been writing and for more than 45 years on religious and historical subjects.

He has published more than 100 books and innumerable articles.

Mr, Pelton proudly claims a heritage going all the way back to well before the War for American Independence.

One of Mr. Pelton's ancestors John Rogers came to America on the Mayflower and was one of 41 signers of the *Mayflower Compact*.

Another, John Smith was one of the founders of Jamestown.

Peleg Pelton served as the fifer in the Continental Army at age 17 during the Battle of Saratoga (1777) and again in Yorktown (1781).

Captain Peter Hager was Commander of the Old Stone Fort in Schoharie, New York, in 1780.

Mr. Pelton is a charter member of the General Henry Knox chapter of Sons of the Revolution (SOR) in Knoxville Tennessee and Sons of the American Revolution (SAR) as well.